LOOKING AT CHRISTMAS

Steven Banks

I0139512

BROADWAY PLAY PUBLISHING INC
New York
www.broadwayplaypublishing.com
info@broadwayplaypublishing.com

LOOKING AT CHRISTMAS
© Copyright 2010 by Steven Banks

Cover photo by Joan Marcus
I S B N: 978-0-88145-687-5
First printing: November 2016

Book design: Marie Donovan
Typographic controls: Adobe InDesign
Typeface: Palatino
Printed and bound in the U S A

LOOKING AT CHRISTMAS received its world premiere at The Flea Theater (Producing Director, Carol Ostrow; Managing Director, Beth Dembrow) in New York City on 20 November 2010. The cast and creative contributors were:

CHARMIAN .... Allison Buck
JOHN .... Michael Micalizzi
MRS CLAUS, MODEL, DELLA .... Betsy Lippitt
ELF .... Christian Adam Jacobs
SCROOGE, JOHNNY PAT .... Jack Corcoran
TINY TIM, CATHLEEN, MARY .... Turna Mete
SNOWMAN, JOSEPH .... Raul Sigmund Julia
JIM, BUDDY .... John Russo
BETTY, LITTLE MATCH GIRL .... Holly Chou

Director .... Jim Simpson
Set design .... Kate Sinclair Foster
Lighting design .... Jeanette Oi-Suk Yew
Costume design .... Gabriel Berry
Sound design .... Jill BC Du Boff
Technical & production consultant .... Kyle Chepulis

The author would like to thank Charles Dickens, O Henry, Hans Christian Anderson, and a fisherman named Luke for their help on this play.

Dedicated to Mom and Dad,
who knew how to put on a damn good Christmas.

"To dash it like a Christmas comedy:
Some carry-tale, some please-man, some slight zany"
William Shakespeare

Scene One

(Lights up.)

(No curtain)

(Empty stage except for a small riser upstage right. Perhaps colored Christmas tree lights framing the stage. Or tree ornaments hanging on the sides. Maybe a large, simple window-like frame, framing the proscenium.)

(A New York sidewalk)

(Upstage area is dimly lit with white lights. Downstage area is brighter with some color, as if reflecting from a store window.)

(Standing center, JOHN, 25–30, in a winter coat, scarf. Messenger bag style briefcase over his shoulder. He is talking on a cell phone, mid-conversation.)

JOHN: *(Pacing, upset)* …Yeah, this is gonna go down as one of the great Christmas Eve's of all time…I couldn't believe it either… No. I am not kidding you. Do I sound like I'm kidding you? …Sarah came in my office, said "John, can we talk for a minute?" And then she closes the door. Soon as she closed the door I knew it… She said exactly what I thought she'd say…I said, "Okay", and then she left and then I left… *(Sighs)* Just been walking around. *(Stops to look up to see where he is)* I'm in front of Bloomingdale's. *(Looks out center)* Looking at the Christmas windows. How pathetic is that? …Good question. I don't know. Get drunk. Hit somebody. Jump off the Empire State building.

Or maybe all three at the same time…No, thanks, it's getting late, I'm just gonna go home to the apartment I can't afford anymore…I'm not exactly in a party mood…Elliot, I just got fired. I don't want to sing Joy To The World and I don't want to drink egg nog and put tinsel on a tree. I don't want Christmas. Okay?

(A woman, CHARMIAN, [pronounced KAR-mee-en], mid-twenties, enters, also dressed for cold weather; a winter coat, scarf, gloves, a knitted wool hat in the shape of a dog's face, with long ears hanging down. Purse over her shoulder. Holding a piece of paper. As she moves downstage her eyes get wider as she takes it he window.)

JOHN: *(On phone)* I'm not gonna change my mind… Yeah. Sure. Bye.

(As JOHN hangs up, CHARMIAN stops center, looks out at audience [window].)

CHARMIAN: *(To herself)* Holy shit. *(Sees JOHN, a little embarrassed)* Sorry. It's just, these are amazingly amazing.

(JOHN politely smiles at CHARMIAN.)

JOHN: Mmm hmm.

CHARMIAN: I've seen them on T V, but it doesn't compare. They're fantastic. You probably see them all the time? No big thing? Kinda boring?

(JOHN shrugs.)

CHARMIAN: They said to come late at night to avoid the crowds. *(Back at window)* I just want to eat this whole window. Doesn't it look delicious? That reindeer is *totally* made of candy canes. There're like a *million* candy canes…I picture some twenty-year-old intern on ten cups of coffee, chain smoking cigarettes and going crazy with a glue gun all night: *(Mimes using a glue gun)* "I hate my job, I hate my job, I hate my job". *(Moves to Mrs. Claus, a "new" window)* You wouldn't think

Mrs Claus would wear a mini skirt at her age, would
you? But, if I had legs like that I'd wear a mini-skirt
all the time…I bet it's totally distracting for the elves.
Everything's right at their eye level. That elf looks
really distracted. And kinda depressed, don'cha think?

JOHN: Maybe he had a bad day at work?

CHARMIAN: But, he's an elf. He can't have a bad day
at work. His job is to delight children of all ages. And
he can't do it when he looks like Mister McSour Puss.
(Looks closer and carefully) Mrs Claus looks like she's
had work. I mean, she looks *really good* for her age. Isn't
she like seven hundred years old? Or *maybe* this is *not*
the first Mrs Claus. Did Santa get a trophy wife? We
would have heard, right? So, did you come to look at
the windows?

JOHN: No. I had to work late.

CHARMIAN: Really? On Christmas Eve? Is your name
Bob Cratchit?

JOHN: *(A small smile)* No. It's John.

(CHARMIAN extends her hand, they shake hands.)

CHARMIAN: I'm Charmian. Pronounced Charmian.

JOHN: How do you spell that?

CHARMIAN: C-h-a-r-m-i-a-n. The "h" is silent and
totally useless.

JOHN: Does it mean something?

CHARMIAN: It means my parents wanted to saddle
me with a weird name so people would ask annoying
questions. Just kidding. They just liked the name.
It's the name of the woman who played the eldest
daughter in *The Sound of Music*. Charmian Carr.
Y'know: *(Half sings)*
I am sixteen,

Going on 17,
I love a Nazi youth.

(JOHN's *not sure of what to make of this person, but he's intrigued.*)

JOHN: Do you like it?

CHARMIAN: *The Sound of Music*? Ye-ah.

JOHN: No, I meant your name.

CHARMIAN: Oh. Yeah, I do. You like yours?

JOHN: What's there to like? It's just "John".

CHARMIAN: There's a lot of great "John's". Jon Stewart, Jon Hamm, John Lennon, John…Malcovich, uh, John Wilkes Boothe—not so great, John Irving, John Kennedy, two of them, and of course, the very famous John McGrath.

JOHN: Who?

CHARMIAN: *(Like he should know)* John McGrath. From Kokomo, Indiana. The first boy I ever kissed.

JOHN: You're a Hoosier.

CHARMIAN: A what?

JOHN: A Hoosier.

CHARMIAN: *(Blankly)* What's that?

JOHN: You don't know what a—

CHARMIAN: Just kidding. So, what do you do in your office so late on Christmas Eve?

JOHN: Nothing very interesting. Just a job. *(Changing subject)* So, are you on vacation?

CHARMIAN: No. I moved here six months ago. Ever since I was a little girl, I always dreamed that one day I'd come to New York and be a waitress. And my dream came true.

(Off JOHN's *surprised look.* CHARMIAN *laughs.)*

CHARMIAN: No. I want to be an actor. I mean I *am* an actor. I just want someone to hire me. Like all the other nine million actors here.

JOHN: *Nine* million?

CHARMIAN: Actually it's only six hundred and fifty thousand. Y'know, if there were only twenty, it would be a lot easier. Anyway, I've been in my apartment all day, going a little stir crazy, so, I decided I needed to get out and get my New York City Christmas fix.

JOHN: Well. Nice to meet you, Charmian.

CHARMIAN: *(Pleased)* Hey! You said it right the first time. Nobody does that.

JOHN: Well. Enjoy the windows.

(JOHN starts to walk away, CHARMIAN pulls out a piece of paper and gestures for him to come back.)

CHARMIAN: Oh, could you— *(Showing him paper with map of stores)* It says I should start here at Bloomingdale's, then Barney's, Bergdorf Goodman, Saks, Lord & Taylor, and the big grand finale at Macy's. How long would that take?

JOHN: Depends on how long you want to look.

(CHARMIAN looks back at window.)

CHARMIAN: I could look at this forever.

JOHN: Then it'll take you a really long time.

CHARMIAN: So, can I just walk to them all?

JOHN: Yeah. I've never done it. But, it's a nice night. You look physically fit.

CHARMIAN: So, do you have to get back to Mrs Cratchit and Tiny Tim?

JOHN: Huh? *(Getting it)* Oh. No. There's no Mrs Cratchit. Or Tiny Tim. I hope.

CHARMIAN: Um… Do you want to go with me? To look at the windows? I'm going to a party, later, but if you want to—I know. It's Christmas Eve. You've probably got big, fancy plans.

JOHN: Actually a friend of mine's having a party.

CHARMIAN: Oh. Okay. I just thought it'd be more fun to go with someone. I'm not—I just want to look at the windows. I'm not a weirdo. Am I coming off like a weirdo?

(Beat)

JOHN: No.

CHARMIAN: Good.

JOHN: Well, have a ---

CHARMIAN: Y'know, I might get famous someday and you could say, "I once looked at Christmas windows with the next Meryl Streep"…Or whoever you think is a great actor.

JOHN: Sorry. I better get going. But, have a good time.

CHARMIAN: Okay. Merry Christmas— Oh! Are you Jewish? Or do you like hate and despise Christmas? Should I not say that?

JOHN: I'm not. It's okay. Merry Christmas.

(JOHN walks off left. CHARMIAN calls after him.)

CHARMIAN: *(Sings)*
And a Happy New Year!

(CHARMIAN watches JOHN go for a moment.)

CHARMIAN: *(Under her breath, embarrassed)* Oh my God. *(Softly, mocking/imitating herself)* "You could say, 'I once looked at Christmas windows with the next Meryl Streep'". *(Shakes her head)* What a tool— And I sang. I sang! *(She sighs. Looks at window. Then pulls out her map, looks at it.)*

(JOHN *returns, comes up behind* CHARMIAN, *she doesn't see him.*)

JOHN: Okay.

CHARMIAN: *(Startled)* Oh!

JOHN: Sorry. I can get to my party fashionably late.

CHARMIAN: Yeah? Awesome. What made you change your mind?

JOHN: *(Shrugs)* You might be the next Meryl Streep.

CHARMIAN: I might. Hey, you're not an axe murderer are you?

JOHN: No.

CHARMIAN: Phew.

JOHN: *(Points to window)* You done with this one?

CHARMIAN: *(Looks at window for a second, then back to* JOHN*)* Yes. *(Raising her hand)* Lay on MacDuff! *(Suddenly embarrassed)* Sorry. Lame. Cliche actor thing to say. But, just so you know, everyone always says, "*Lead* on, MacDuff" and everyone is wrong. Mr. Macbeth never utters those words.

JOHN: I thought it was bad luck to say "Macbeth"?

CHARMIAN: Macbeth-Macbeth-Macbeth-Macbeth. When people say, "The Scottish play" I just want to hit them. You know what I say to people on opening nights? "Good luck, Macbeth." *(Smiles)* They get really mad.

JOHN: I bet they do. Okay. Well. "Lay on Macduff".

CHARMIAN: "…and damn'd be him that first cries, 'Hold, enough!'" *(To* JOHN*)* Which way?

JOHN: *(Points off)* This way. *(To window)* Bye, Mrs Claus. You look fabulous. It was worth every penny.

(*As* CHARMIAN *and* JOHN *walk off, over her shoulder…*)

CHARMIAN: And watch out for that creepy elf.

(*Music:* Jolly Old Saint Nicholas. *[Note: All music can be recorded or a live piano or off-stage actors singing])*

(*Lights fade*)

Scene Two

(*Music continues.*)

(*A short moment of darkness. These transitions should be as quick as possible.*)

(*Lights up; very colorful and bright.*)

(*Music slowly fades as scene begins.*)

(*Standing center are* MRS CLAUS, *20s-30s, but with white hair, wire-rimmed glasses, red mini-skirt, with white fur lining, wide black belt, boots and a Santa hat.*)

(*Next to her is an* ELF *[actor on his knees], pointed ears, rosy cheeks, wearing elf costume; tights, short top, belt, hat, shoes with curled up tips; holding a toy train and a screw driver.*)

(*They are both posing as if mannequins.*)

(*Beat*)

(*They relax.* ELF *looks off to where* CHARMIAN *and* JOHN *exited.*)

ELF: Hey? Mrs C? You hear what that girl said?

MRS CLAUS: Yes. And I have not had any "work" done. It's the egg nog. It's wonderful for the skin.

ELF: No, no, I meant "Watch out for that creepy elf". She better watch out for that creepy guy. Y'know, I bet he takes innocent young women to look at Christmas windows and then strangles then with tinsel… Which would not be easy. (*Getting into it*) Or-or maybe he stabs them with a sharpened candy cane. Then he eats the candy cane and there's no evidence!

MRS CLAUS: You are so silly! He looked like a nice young man to me. He was cute.

ELF: Yeah? I bet Hitler looked cute some times. When he got his moustache and his hair just right.

MRS CLAUS: Maybe he just wants to look at the windows? Maybe there's a romance in store?

ELF: Okay, okay, let's say he's not Ted Bundy. Who, incidentally, I made a jack in the box for when he was five. Cute kid. Who knew? Anyway, I don't think there's any romance in the future for those two.

MRS CLAUS: There's always a chance they could fall in love and live happily ever after.

ELF: Mrs. C, I think you put a little too much nutmeg in your egg nog. *Nobody* lives happily ever after.

MRS CLAUS: Oh, really? What about Santa and me? We've been happily married for six hundred and twenty-nine years.

ELF: It could still fall apart. And may I be honest? I don't think Mister Ho Ho Ho is good enough for you.

MRS CLAUS: What? He's the epitome of "good". He's brought joy to millions of people for hundreds of years.

ELF: Yeah, yeah, so have lots of people: Shakespeare, Beethoven, Cher. Look, let me get right down to it. Does Santa…satisfy you as a woman? I know he has some weight issues.

MRS CLAUS: That's none of your business!

ELF: Well, I'd like to make it my business. You need someone younger. And shorter. And y'know what they say; "Once you go elf, you never go back on the shelf".

MRS CLAUS: …That makes absolutely no sense.

ELF: I know. "Elf" is a hard rhyme.

MRS CLAUS: Why are you interested in me? There are hundreds of lovely female elves up here.

ELF: Short women don't do it for me. It's a problem. I tried. I was dating Trixie, the tallest elf I could find; a strapping three feet two inches. Everything was terrific until I found out she was also "dating" Jack Frost, The Grinch, Rudolph, The Sugar Plum Fairy—

MRS CLAUS: Wait a minute, everyone knows the Sugar Plum Fairy is—

ELF: I know! Trixie likes a challenge. The point is, Mrs. C, I'm only attracted to beautiful, tall, pre-maturely grey haired women who wear wire-rimmed glasses.

MRS CLAUS: Well, you need to find a new type. Nothing's ever going to happen. Period.

ELF: Is it the pointy ears? The curly shoes? The rosacea?

MRS CLAUS: Get back to work. And if you bring this up again I will call security.

(ELF *sighs. Fiddles with toy train. Looks out window*)

ELF: Well, I hope nothing horrible happens to that girl when she's out with the Christmas Candy Cane Killer.

MRS CLAUS: Y'know, Mr. Gloomy Doomy, maybe something good will actually happen? It is Christmas Eve. Surprising things have been known to occur.

ELF: (*Thinks, smiles*) You mean like virile, handsome elves and gorgeous, statuesque women having a deep, meaningful relationship and doing the nasty behind the defective teddy bears?

MRS CLAUS: (*Yells off*) Security!

(*The* ELF *raises his hands, afraid, and then frantically works on the train.*)

(*Black out*)

(*Music:* Deck The Halls)

(Lights fade.)

Scene Three

(Music fades as lights come up.)

(Another sidewalk. CHARMIAN *and* JOHN *upstage.)*

CHARMIAN: How long've you lived in New York?

JOHN: Too long.

CHARMIAN: You don't like it?

JOHN: I used to. I think I'm done with this city. People come here and they all want to make it big, but the truth is, ninety-nine per cent of them fail. I mean, it's great when you first get here, it's this big, scary, exciting place with all these infinite possibilities, but after awhile it just beats you up and wears you out and grinds you down.

CHARMIAN: Are you the guy who invented the "I Love New York" T-shirt?

JOHN: I'm sorry. I didn't mean to— You shouldn't listen to me. I had a bad day. I got fired.

CHARMIAN: Fired? On Christmas Eve? That should be illegal.

JOHN: Yeah. Look, I should go home. I'm not the best Christmas window looking partner…person… whatever, right now. I don't want to spoil your night. I'm sorry. It was nice to meet you.

*(*JOHN *shakes* CHARMIAN *hand.)*

CHARMIAN: But, we just got started.

JOHN: I know, but, I should go. You'll have more fun alone. Trust me.

CHARMIAN: But, I don't want to look at these all by myself. That would be *really* pathetic and…and sad…

and I'd be so depressed I'd probably jump off the
Empire State Building. *(Nods)* And, I might land on top
of a really cute puppy or the person who was going
to cure cancer and flatten them like a pancake and it
would be all your fault. You would forever be known
as The Man Kept Cancer From Being Cured. Could you
live with that?

JOHN: *(He's won over, reluctantly smiles.)* No... Okay.

*(CHARMIAN and JOHN move down stage and look at
window. She makes a face of disgust.)*

CHARMIAN: Oh my god. What is this? Charles Dickens
on crack?

JOHN: Barney's is famous for their strange windows.

CHARMIAN: This isn't a Christmas Carol. This is
a Christmas abomination. This will give children
nightmares. This will give *me* nightmares. I'm sorry.
This is so wrong. Ebeneezer Scrooge and Tiny Tim
as zombies? Seriously? *(Shaking her head)* Okay, the
execution is superb. I will give you that. But the
idea? Nay. I do not like this window. I mean, Charles
Dickens is going to climb out of his grave and beat this
person to death with that bloody leg stump that Tiny
Tim is using as a crutch. If this is the first time a little
kid is exposed to *A Christmas Carol* and then they read
the original, they're going to ask, "Mommy? When is
Mister Scrooge going to start eating people?"

JOHN: I don't know. If I was a kid, I'd think it looked
pretty cool. And I wouldn't have minded getting a
zombie Tiny Tim action figure for Christmas.

CHARMIAN: You are so weird. What was the best
Christmas gift you ever got?

JOHN: The best? Uh, I got this transformer-robot once
that was really amazing; you could shoot rockets out of
its eyes. I used to terrorize my sister's Barbie with it.

CHARMIAN: How kind of you...*I* never had a Barbie.

JOHN: Really? I thought every little girl had a Barbie.

CHARMIAN: You were wrong, John. My mother didn't think Barbie was an appropriate female role model. So, Barbies were forbidden in my house. If a friend brought one over, poor little Barbie had to stay outside.

JOHN: Are you kidding?

CHARMIAN: I don't joke about things like this. I can remember playing with my best friend, Nancy Gruber, in my room and looking out the window and seeing her poor little Barbie, sitting outside on the grass...

(CHARMIAN *poses, stiff, like a Barbie doll, with arms, bent at elbow, a big, frozen smile on her face. She holds the pose.* JOHN *smiles.*)

CHARMIAN: ...she was smiling, but I knew, that inside, she was crying.

JOHN: You do a very good Barbie.

CHARMIAN: *(Matter of fact)* I know. *(She relaxes out of pose.)*

JOHN: Did you want a Barbie?

CHARMIAN: In the worst possible way.

JOHN: What was the best gift you ever got?

CHARMIAN: *(Thinks)* I don't know. I don't think I've gotten my best Christmas gift, yet. I give great gifts. Last year, I gave my boyfriend an awesome gift.

JOHN: *(Disappointed to hear she has a boyfriend)* Oh.

CHARMIAN: He's back in Indiana.

JOHN: *(Not as bad as he thought)* Oh.

CHARMIAN: We're "sort of engaged".

JOHN: *(Worse than he thought)* Oh.

CHARMIAN: There's no ring. Or date. Or anything.

JOHN: *(Maybe there's a chance…)* Oh. Well, "sort of congratulations" to you and Mr. Indiana.

CHARMIAN: Thanks. So, I gave him this gift ---

(JOHN's cell rings. He looks to see who it is.)

JOHN: Excuse me. I should take this.

CHARMIAN: Take.

John steps away to talk and Charmian checks her phone and then looks at window.

JOHN: *(Answers phone)* Hey, Elliot…I'm okay, I'm fine… It sounds like a great party… Who's Heather?… *(A sly smile)* Oh, yeah… Yes, they are quite spectacular. But, have you ever talked to her? She thought F. Scott Fitzgerald was the name of a band. *(He listens for a bit, getting interested, smiles)*

She really said that? …And you're sure she meant me? …Well, I have some stuff to do, but I'll be over later…Yeah. See ya. *(He hangs up. Back to* CHARMIAN. *Explaining)* My friend, who's having the party.

CHARMIAN: Do you need to go?

JOHN: Not yet.

CHARMIAN: Okay. So, anyway, I gave my boyfriend this awesome gift. He's Irish. Way Irish. Michael Seamus McCarthy— So, anyway, last Christmas I had this quilt made, with his family crest. It was amazing. I spent a lot of money. And you know what he gave me? U2's Greatest Hits. An effing C D! Who even buys C Ds? And it wasn't even the double disk version with the extra songs no one really wants. *(Offhandedly)* I threw it at him. *(Nods to window)* So, are you ready to bid farewell to this horrific desecration of a classic piece of Christmas literature and move on?

JOHN: Sure.

CHARMIAN: *(To window)* Mister Scrooge, Mister Tim, my condolences.

(CHARMIAN and JOHN walk off.)

CHARMIAN: I don't even like U2.

(Lights fade out.)

(Music: Singers or Victorian instrumental version of God Rest Ye Merry Gentlemen.*)*

Scene Four

(Music fades out as lights come up.)

(Standing center, TINY TIM, in tattered and torn Victorian outfit. He is using a bloody leg stump, with pant leg and shoe attached, as a crutch and munching on a severed hand.)

(Next to TINY TIM is SCROOGE, long, white hair, spectacles, torn long white nightshirt, slippers, nightcap. An eye hanging out of its socket or a bite out of his cheek.)

(Both faces are pale and decaying, maybe wearing white contact lenses.)

(They speak with English accents. SCROOGE—refined, stuffy, pretentious, quick to outrage, think John Cleese. TINY TIM—Cockney.)

TINY TIM: *(Looking out window)* Oi. She was a nice piece of puddin'.

SCROOGE: Yes. She seemed a spirited, intelligent, young woman; rather unfortunate for the gentleman accompanying her that she is already betrothed.

TINY TIM: *(Grins)* That's not gonna stop 'im. Wouldn't stop me. All is fair in love and war, right? She ain't betrothed; no bloody ring? No weddin' date? Irish wanker. I wouldn't mind gettin' in her saddle and takin' a ride.

SCROOGE: I beg your pardon? Aren't you a bit young for such thoughts?

TINY TIM: No! I'm just short for me age. Combined with the fact I'm a cripple. People make erroneous assumptions because of me affliction. I'm in the pubescent state, I've got natural urges just like anybody else and my reproductive organs are in perfect working order—

SCROOGE: Enough! I don't wish to stand here discussing your reproductive organs!

TINY TIM: Fine. All I'm sayin' is I fancy her.

SCROOGE: She had her charms. I suppose.

TINY TIM: "I suppose"? You wouldn't mind stuffin' her crumpet. If you're still capable, that is.

SCROOGE: I beg your pardon! I am advanced in age, but I am in very good health! Someday you'll be my age.

TINY TIM: No, I won't. I'll always be a kid. And you'll always be an old man. We'll never bloody change.

SCROOGE: (Sighs) True. Such is our curse. (Brightening) But, also our blessing! We are immortal. And we shall remain so as long as our story is told, *properly*, in the correct fashion, not in this utterly ridiculous setting, as that intelligent young girl pointed out!

TINY TIM: (Groans) Oh, Christ, 'ere he goes again.

SCROOGE: (Disgusted) Zombies! Humbug! This is absurd!

TINY TIM: Who says so? We are iconic characters in a timeless story. A true artist can interpret us any way they want, long as they stay true to the central conceit of the story. They do Shakespeare plays in different time periods, different interpretations, why not us? Doesn't bother Shakespeare.

SCROOGE: How do you know?

TINY TIM: I heard. *(He takes a bite of hand.)*

SCROOGE: Humbug! If Mister Dickens had wanted to write about animated corpses devouring their fellow man he would have!

TINY TIM: I wish the old bastard had!

SCROOGE: Hold your tongue! You need to show your creator some respect!

TINY TIM: Respect?! *(Points to his leg)* He made me a bloody cripple!

SCROOGE: Yes, but, you get better in the end.

TINY TIM: Right. Very last page. For a large part of the story I'm hobblin' around and then I die.

SCROOGE: *(Not to be bested)* I die, too. And I see my own grave! That is not a pleasant experience!

TINY TIM: Right, but it all works out at the end and everybody loves you.

SCROOGE: True. But, you get the last line. The *best* line. The most famous line.

TINY TIM: It's the only thing I say in the whole bleedin' story! One flippin' line!

SCROOGE: You say it twice.

TINY TIM: Twice! Oh la dee dah! Five bloody words! You got inner monologues, soliloquies, you're talkin' all the time. You're 'amlet compared to me! I'm sick of that bloody line. It's a nice thought, but if the truth be told, God doesn't bless us everyone. He's a very arbitrary deity. Millions of innocent people die and suffer and get tortured and murdered and he does bloody nothing—

SCROOGE: Stop it! That is blasphemous!

(SCROOGE raises his hand as if to strike TINY TIM, then freezes, his hand mid-air.)

TINY TIM: Are you actually gonna strike one of literatures most beloved characters? Who 'appens to be a kid? A little, tiny kid? A little, tiny *crippled* kid?

(SCROOGE *slowly lowers his hand and regains his composure.*

SCROOGE: Forgive me. I lost my temper. It shall not happen again. *(Beat)* But I don't care what you say, it is a magnificent line. *(Wistfully)* I wish it were mine.

TINY TIM: I wish that piece of puddin'd come back. *(He offers the hand he has been snacking on.)* Want a bite? Ain't bad.

SCROOGE: *(Disgusted)* Humbug!

(Music: God Rest Ye Merry Gentlemen*)*

(Lights Fade.)

Scene Five

(Music fades as lights come up.)

(Another sidewalk.)

(As CHARMIAN *and* JOHN *enter:)*

CHARMIAN: "Only one thing in the world could've dragged me away from the soft glow of electric sex gleaming in the window."

*(*JOHN *stops dead in his tracks. Looks at* CHARMIAN. *Baffled)*

JOHN: I have no idea.

CHARMIAN: Yes. Very famous Christmas movie. Okay, you'll get it from this: "Fra-geel-lay. That must be Italian."

(Off JOHN's *blank look)*

CHARMIAN: Oh my god, this is your last chance. If you don't get it from this, you get no presents this year. "You'll shoot your eye out, kid! Ho! Ho!—"

JOHN: Oh, right. *A Christmas Story.*

CHARMIAN: Correct. Charmian's Greatest Christmas Movies of All Time Number Four: *(As a boy)* "I wish I had a million dollars— Hot dog!"

JOHN: *(Raises his hand)* It's *A Wonderful Life.* My parents forced me to watch that every Christmas. Y'know, I always felt bad that Jimmy Stewart wants to be an architect and see the world and he's stuck in that little town his whole life. It's depressing.

CHARMIAN: I think you missed the entire point of the film.
Okay. Number three: *(Imitates Doctor Finklestein/William Hickey from "Nightmare Before Christmas")* "That's twice this month you've slipped deadly nightshade into my tea and run off."

(JOHN baffled again, shakes his head.)

CHARMIAN: *Nightmare Before Christmas!*

JOHN: Oh, yeah. That was a strange movie.

CHARMIAN: *(Mutters)* You're a strange movie. Okay. Number two: *(Stage whisper)* "You stink. You smell like beef and cheese. You don't smell like Santa."

JOHN: That's the one with Vince Vaughn, about Santa's brother.

CHARMIAN: *(Disdainfully) Fred Claus*? No! It's from *Elf.* I hate Fred Claus. My boyfriend loves that movie. He watches it all the time. He forced me to watch *it.* We almost broke up. All right, John. Final movie. Number one: *(As Ratso the muppet)* "Light the lamp, not the rat, light the lamp, not the rat! Put me out, put me out, put me out!"

JOHN: I have no idea.

CHARMIAN: *(Like everyone should know) The Muppet Christmas Carol.*

JOHN: I never saw it.

CHARMIAN: Well, that's just shameful. Your parents should've been reported to the Christmas Police. When do you open your gifts?

JOHN: *(Wary to answer)* …Christmas morning?

CHARMIAN: *That* is the correct answer. Anyone who opens their gifts on Christmas Eve should be sent to Christmas Jail.

JOHN: My boss lets her kids open one gift on Christmas Eve.

CHARMIAN: Those kids are gonna be seriously 'effed up.

JOHN: *(Realizing)* I guess she's my ex-boss now.

CHARMIAN: So, what do you do? I mean, you don't have to tell me if you're like a spy or an assassin or a mime.

JOHN: I'm a writer.

CHARMIAN: Impressive.

JOHN: Don't be impressed. I write books for kids.

CHARMIAN: I love children's literature. That's awesome. I've read all the Harry Potter's. Twice. I love Roald Dahl—

JOHN: No, no, I don't write *those* kind of kid's books. I write…well, up until a few hours ago, I *wrote*, books based on cartoons.

CHARMIAN: Oh…Huh?

JOHN: They make a cartoon for T V, and then I write a book version of the story. Thirty-six pages. A hundfred and ten words maximum. I'm sure you've read *The Vampire Sharks Very Special Day.*

CHARMIAN: Uh, not yet. But… That's a great way to get kids to read.

JOHN: Yeah. That's what I've been telling myself for four years.

(CHARMIAN *and* JOHN *walk downstage to look at window.*)

CHARMIAN: Okay. Are we really supposed to believe that woman actually made that snowman?

JOHN: Yes. She was walking through the forest, in the dead of winter, in her four-inch high heels and evening gown and decided to stop and make a snowman. Happens all the time.

CHARMIAN: I made the most awesome snowman once, when I was like five or six. I fell in love with that snowman. I wanted to marry him and have snow babies. I'd sit outside and talk to him for hours and dress him up and eat my lunch with him. He was my first boyfriend. And like all my subsequent boyfriends, one day I went out to play with him and he had melted away.

(JOHN *looks closer at window.*)

JOHN: Weird.

CHARMIAN: I was.

JOHN: No. Not that— (*Points at window*) She really looks like my ex-girlfriend.

CHARMIAN: (*Impressed*) Way to go, John. Hottie.

JOHN: (*Nods*) She was. She was also psychotic. And shallow. And completely self-absorbed.

CHARMIAN: The hotties always are. Kidding… Well, not really.

JOHN: She broke up with me last Christmas.

CHARMIAN: Wow. Christmas is not your holiday, is it?

JOHN: Apparently not.

CHARMIAN: So, do you do any other kind of writing?

JOHN: Yeah. I specialize in writing novels that no one wants to publish. I've done it three times now. I was half-way through a fourth book and decided to put it out of its misery.

CHARMIAN: You quit? But, what if you were writing the Great American Novel?

JOHN: F. Scott Fitzgerald already wrote the great American novel.

CHARMIAN: *Great Gatsby?* Or *The Last Tycoon?*

(JOHN smiles, intrigued.)

CHARMIAN: Because if you say Gatsby we may have an argument on our hands. Gatsby is great, no pun intended, but, I actually prefer *The Last Tycoon.*

JOHN: *(Very pleased)* You are so wrong.

(CHARMIAN's cell goes off. The ring tone is U2's "But I Still Haven't Found What I'm Looking For".)

CHARMIAN: Sorry. *(Re ring tone)* My boyfriend put this in, I don't know how to change it—

(CHARMIAN moves to right to talk and JOHN moves downstage left to look at window and pulls out his phone and pretends to text…and listens to her conversation.)

CHARMIAN: *(On cell)* Hi, Michael… Great. I'm out looking at Christmas windows. They're amazing… Yes. It's totally safe. I'm with— *(Glances over at JOHN)* —lots of people are around. *(Looks up)* What are you doing?… *(Exasperated)* Oh my God. How many times can you watch that stupid movie?—Never mind. Oh, hey, remember that T V thing I read for last week? … Yes, you do…Michael, I told you like three times—

Doesn't matter. I didn't get it… What? Did you just
say "good"? …Why would you say that? …I know you
want me to come home— Can we talk about this later?
It's getting cold…I'll call you later. Bye.

*(CHARMIAN hangs up. Walks over to JOHN, who pretends to
be texting and looks up.)*

JOHN: Everything good in Indiana?

CHARMIAN: *(Puts on a smile)* Perfect.

JOHN: So, how do you work out the boyfriend there
and you here situation? Does he come out to visit?

CHARMIAN: No. He hates New York. Even though he's
never been. He didn't want me to come. He thinks I
should be an actor back in Kokomo. Which I guess I
could, if I wanted to do *"Oklahoma!"* at The Eat, Drink
and Be Musical Dinner Theater… So, we made a deal;
I have six months to get a really great part or become
famous or something.

JOHN: Six months? That's not very long.

CHARMIAN: I know.

JOHN: What if nothing happens?

CHARMIAN: *(Sighs, then quietly…)* Ohhhhhh— *(Into
singing, dead pan)*
—Ooooooooo-klahoma
Where the wind comes sweepin' down the plain.

JOHN: I had a girlfriend that said if I hadn't sold a book
in a year I should give up writing and do something
else. I gave her up.

CHARMIAN: Good for you.

JOHN: Now I think I she was right and I should've done
something else.

CHARMIAN: Like what?

JOHN: Axe murderer?

CHARMIAN: I bet that doesn't pay very well.

JOHN: Yeah. And they're probably outsourcing it.

(CHARMIAN *mimes answering a phone.*)

CHARMIAN: *(Indian accent)* Hello? May I help you, please? Whose head would you like me to cut off with axe?

JOHN: *(Laughs, then…)* Once, for Christmas, I gave her a novel I had written. It was all about her, basically a two hundred and forty page love letter.

CHARMIAN: She must've loved that.

JOHN: No. She got mad. She thought it was lame because I hadn't spent any money on her.

CHARMIAN: Did she throw it at you?

JOHN: No. But I felt like throwing it at her.

CHARMIAN: What'd she get you for Christmas?

JOHN: Hmm? I don't remember.

CHARMIAN: Well, if a guy ever wrote me a book I'd basically fall in love with him on the spot—

(Awkward moment)

(CHARMIAN *turns back to window.*)

CHARMIAN: I really want your her dress. I don't know where I'd wear it, but I would love to know it was hanging in my closet.

JOHN: You could wear it when you go to the Oscars.

CHARMIAN: Yeah. Right. If I ever was nominated Meryl *Streep* would be too. And she'd win for the nine millionth time. *(Quietly considers)* Maybe I should kill the bitch? Just kidding. I couldn't kill The Streep…I love her too much. *(Turns to* JOHN*)* Major Embarrassing Confession: I've had a picture of her up on my wall since I was eleven.

JOHN: Well, I had a picture of F Scott Fitzgerald on my wall since I was fifteen. My Uma Thurman poster came down and up he went. My dad was a little concerned till I explained who it was.

CHARMIAN: I always wanted somebody to put my picture up on their wall someday. I mean, besides my mother or my Gramma. Hey, if someone needed to find a bathroom, around here, where would you think it might be?

JOHN: Uh, oh, let me check. *(He takes out his cell phone.)*

CHARMIAN: Is there an I Need To Pee In New York app?

JOHN: Probably. But, I have a friend who knows where every decent public rest room in the city is. And rates them.

CHARMIAN: Handy friend.

JOHN: With a very small bladder. *(Into phone)* Hey, Elliot, I'm at 5th and 58th, where's the nearest— *(Smiles at* CHARMIAN*)* ...Thanks...Yeah, I'll be there in a little bit...I'm looking at Christmas windows with the next Meryl Streep.

*(*CHARMIAN, *looking out at "window", smiles to herself.)*

JOHN: *(Into phone)* See ya. *(Hangs up)* Plaza Hotel. He gives it a nine. One of his favorites. Excellent soap.

CHARMIAN: *(To window)* Adieu, Mister Snowman and beautiful perfect sexy woman.

(As CHARMIAN *and* JOHN *walk off.)*

CHARMIAN: Where do you stand on the mince pie question? Do you eat it or do you bury it in the back yard?

(Lights fade.)

(Music: Jazzy or contemporary version of Jingle Bells *or* Deck The Halls.*)*

Scene Six

(Music fades as lights come up.)

(A SNOWMAN, *top hat, scarf, pipe, black coal eyes, carrot nose and boots.)*

(Female MODEL, *20s, sullen, gorgeous; wearing a slinky, sexy, glamorous evening gown, a small evening bag over her shoulder.)*

(She opens her purse and digs through it.)

(She speaks with Russian accent.)

MODEL: This totally suck. Where is cigarettes?

SNOWMAN: That was a really cute couple.

MODEL: *(Still digging in purse)* She was retarded. He was cute. Why no cigarettes?

*(*SNOWMAN *holds out his pipe.)*

SNOWMAN: Would you like my pipe?

MODEL: *(Looks up)* You got the crack?

SNOWMAN: No. Sorry. Just bubbles.

MODEL: *(Considers)* Never done bubbles. *(She takes the pipe. Blows some bubbles)* That suck.

*(*MODEL *hands pipe back to* SNOWMAN *disgustedly.)*

SNOWMAN: So, what do you think that guy and girl are gonna do tonight?

MODEL: Don't care.

SNOWMAN: I was just wondering.

MODEL: Then I tell: She take him home. He do the sex with her. She never see asshole again.

SNOWMAN: You really think so?

MODEL: Yes, snowman. Always happen. I'm hot.
I party. I do good in the bed. What else guy want?
(Disgusted) Is pointless.

SNOWMAN: What's pointless?

MODEL: Everything. This. Us. Them. Who cares she
become famous actor. Or he big writer. Or they fall in
love. All pointless.

SNOWMAN: I don't think I'm pointless. *(Proudly)* I'm a
snowman. I make people happy. And they have fun
making me and they get exercise and sometimes I'm
even kind of like a work of art.

MODEL: So? Doesn't matter. One day you melt. One
day I die. Gone.

SNOWMAN: That's true…But, while I'm melting, I hope
I can say, "I did good things, I had fun and maybe,
somebody loved me".

MODEL: Whatever.

SNOWMAN: And you're not pointless. You're beautiful.
And people like to look at you because you're beautiful
and they feel good when they look at you, because
you're, uh, beautiful…

MODEL: Nice try. Is sweet.

(MODEL *looks* SNOWMAN *over. Checks his ass)*

SNOWMAN: *(Uncomfortable)* What?

MODEL: You're cute.

SNOWMAN: *(Pleased)* I am?

MODEL: For snowman.

SNOWMAN: Oh. Thanks.

MODEL: Want to have the sex?

SNOWMAN: What?!

MODEL: Never do snowman.

SNOWMAN: *(Embarrassed)* Uh, well, that's really nice of you, but I-I can't.

MODEL: You gay?

SNOWMAN: No.

MODEL: Mormon?

SNOWMAN: No. I…I don't have…

MODEL: Rubbers? I have. *(Goes through purse)* No cigarettes. Plenty rubbers.

SNOWMAN: No, no. I don't have a—

(MODEL *looks up at* SNOWMAN. *He glances down at his crotch. Then she does the same. Then she looks back at him.)*

MODEL: That suck.

(MODEL *and* SNOWMAN *both stare out window for a moment.)*

SNOWMAN: We could hold hands?

MODEL: Are we five?

SNOWMAN: *(Shrugs)* It might be nice.

MODEL: *(Considers, sighs)* Okay.

(SNOWMAN *holds out his hand. Still looking forward* MODEL *holds her hand out and he takes it. They hold hands for a bit.)*

MODEL: Is not as good as the sex.

SNOWMAN: I'm enjoying it.

(A few beats)

MODEL: Okay. Doesn't totally suck.

(Lights fade out.)

(Music: Same as intro to scene.)

Scene Seven

(Music fades as lights come up.)

(Another sidewalk)

(CHARMIAN and JOHN sit upstage on small platform.)

CHARMIAN: —Oh my god. That rest room was bigger than my apartment. And cleaner. I'd rather live in that rest room.

JOHN: Where do you live?

CHARMIAN: Washington Heights, in the world's smallest, darkest, ugliest, coldest, noisiest apartment in New York that I pay way too much for.

JOHN: Yeah, for what I pay here for a 600 square foot studio, back home, in Bethesda, I could rent a two-story house. With a pool.

CHARMIAN: But, wouldn't you rather be a struggling novelist in New York than Bethesda?

JOHN: I don't want to be a struggling novelist anywhere anymore.

CHARMIAN: How long did it take Fitzgerald to make it?

JOHN: His first novel was a best-seller when he was twenty-four.
By the time he was my age he'd had five best sellers.

CHARMIAN: Show off.

JOHN: Later, when he was older, kind of forgotten, not making any money, he said, "There are no second acts in American lives". That's totally fine with me. I just wanted my first act to happen.

CHARMIAN: Maybe you just have a really long first act and it's not over yet.

JOHN: Or maybe this is intermission and it's gonna get worse?

CHARMIAN: My teacher, at college, used to say, "Life is a badly written play, with a horrible ending, but there are some good scenes along the way." Maybe your really good scenes are coming up?

JOHN: *(Ending conversation)* Yeah.

(CHARMIAN and JOHN walk down to look at window.)

CHARMIAN: Hey, it's I Sold My Watch Guy and I Cut My Hair Woman. What's that story called?

JOHN: *The Gift of the Magi.* O Henry.

CHARMIAN: Right. The only story written by a candy bar. Okay, this has always bothered me. She sells her hair to get a watch fob for her husband. Fine. He sells his watch to get her some fancy combs. Her hair is going to grow back. But his watch is not going to grow back. It's gone! He got screwed.

JOHN: Well, I think the point is they were willing to give up some thing they treasured to make the person they loved happy.

CHARMIAN: *(Sighs, mock bored)* Yeah. If you go in for that kind of thing. Love. Making people happy.

JOHN: Would you sell your most prized possession for somebody?

CHARMIAN: I did. I sold my soul to the devil so I could be a big, famous actor. *(Looks down at ground)* And I'm still waiting…I knew it wasn't going to be easy, but I didn't think it would be this hard. Getting rejected all the time, people saying "No, we don't want you."

JOHN: Ever want to quit?

CHARMIAN: Three or four times. A day.

JOHN: Well, I bet Meryl Streep had a tough time when she first came to New York.

CHARMIAN: No, she didn't. The day she arrived in New York she got cast in fifty plays. And she won fifty Tony's. And they gave her a solid gold crown and said, "Behold! You are Queen of Actors!".

JOHN: Really? I didn't know that.

CHARMIAN: Okay. I made some of it up. Except the part about the crown.

JOHN: I bet you'll get your crown someday.

CHARMIAN: I better.

JOHN: Well, I can sympathize. I did a little acting once. Some Shakespeare.

CHARMIAN: Really? John does The Big Bad Bard?

JOHN: Mmm-hmm. I was in a fifteen minute version of Romeo & Juliet at Jefferson Elementary School, 6th grade. I played Romeo, because I was the only boy willing to wear tights. And I got to kiss this girl, Cathy Troller, who was the reason I was willing to put on tights. And so I kissed her. Maybe a little too enthusiastically—

CHARMIAN: Tongues?

JOHN: There's still some controversy about that. Anyway, she punched me in the nose.

CHARMIAN: What'd you do?

JOHN: I got a bloody nose. I bled all over my tights.

CHARMIAN: Must've been some kiss.

JOHN: My only line that I remember is: "If thou dost love, pronounce it faithfully".

CHARMIAN: Actually, that's Juliet's line.

JOHN: It is?

CHARMIAN: O gentle Romeo,
If thou dost love, pronounce it faithfully.

(She looks back at window and then continues, quietly at first, then getting into it, not just reciting, she is quite good.)
Or if thou think'st I am too quickly won,
I'll frown and be perverse an say thee nay,
So thou wilt woo; but else, not for the world
In truth, fair Montague, I am too fond,
And therefore thou mayst think my 'havior light:
But trust me, gentleman, I'll prove more true
Than those that have more cunning to be strange.
I should have been more strange, I must confess,
But that thou overheard'st, ere I was ware,
My true love's passion: therefore pardon me,
And not impute this yielding to light love,
Which the dark night hath so discovered—
(Stops, embarrassed)

Sorry. Didn't mean to go all Shakespeare on you.

JOHN: *(Impressed)* Wow. That was really good.

CHARMIAN: Thanks. Unfortunately it didn't impress the casting director I did it for last week. But, like my Gramma always said, "Shakespeare is dead and you are not." I don't know what that means, but I love it. She died last year, which was really tragic, because she made the best hot chocolate in the world.

JOHN: You like hot chocolate?

CHARMIAN: I *love* hot chocolate.

JOHN: Yeah?

CHARMIAN: *(Mock serious)* No. I hate it. Just kidding. If I could raise people from the dead, I would bring my Gramma back to make me hot chocolate. And then I'd stuff her right back in her coffin because she was a horrible person.

JOHN: Have you ever heard of Monsieur Chocolate? Next to Ambrosia? Near Point Break Bar? On 45th?

CHARMIAN: Uhhh…I've heard of 45th.

JOHN: They make the best hot chocolate in the city. It's not that far away. You want to walk over? Get some?

CHARMIAN: Maybe I do and maybe I do. Will it be open Christmas Eve?

JOHN: We're in New York. The city that never sleeps or stops making hot chocolate.

CHARMIAN: *(To window)* We're getting hot chocolate.

(As CHARMIAN *and* JOHN *walk off, to window)*

CHARMIAN: Sorry you have no hair. Enjoy your fob.

(Lights fade.)

(Music: Singers or Music Box version of O Tannebaum [O Christmas Tree]*)*

Scene Eight

(Music fades out as lights come up.)

*(*JIM, *20s, slicked-back hair, moustache, in plain 1906-era clothes; shirt and tie, vest, shoes. Looking forlornly at a watch fob he holds in his hand.)*

*(*DELLA, *20s, short hair, wearing a long, plain floor-length skirt, white long-sleeved blouse, buttoned to neck, she holds a beautiful tortoise shell comb.)*

(They sit next to each other on a worn love seat or small bench.)

DELLA: *(Smiles, looks out "window")* Beautiful, ain't it?

JIM: *(Looking at fob, wistfully)* Yes. It is.

DELLA: *(Looks at him)* Not the watch fob, Jim. *(Nods out window)* Them.

JIM: *(Indifferent)* Oh. Yes.

DELLA: Do you think they're going to fall in love?

JIM: I suppose.

DELLA: It's so wonderful to see people fall in love.

JIM: Yes. That's the best part.

DELLA: *(Puzzled)* What do you mean "the best part"?

JIM: The beginning. When you first meet someone and you're finding out interesting things about them, telling stories, holding hands for the first time, the first kiss. Everything's new and fresh and exciting. *(Sighs)* But, you can't expect that to last forever. After awhile, you get used to somebody, you know everything about them. That's just the way it is.

DELLA: *(Concerned)* Jim? You ain't bored of me are you?

JIM: *(Almost nodding)* …No.

DELLA: Even after three years?

JIM: Actually it's four. Almost five.

DELLA: But, we won't ever stop loving each other, will we?

JIM: I hope not.

DELLA: You hope?!

JIM: I mean. No. We won't.

(DELLA *turns away from* JIM. *He looks at her hair.*)

JIM: Your hair is really quite short, Della.

DELLA: You hate it, don't you?

JIM: No…it's…fine. How long will it take to grow back?

DELLA: Oh, I figure three years.

JIM: That's a long time.

(DELLA *turns back to face* JIM.)

DELLA: *(Hopeful)* But, I'm still your pretty little girl, ain't I?

JIM: Sure, Della. Just…a different kind of pretty.

DELLA: You do hate it. I look horrible. I look like a boy!

(DELLA *cries.* JIM *studies her a bit.*)

JIM: *(An interesting realization)* Hmm. You do kind of look like a boy.

DELLA: Oh, Jim, I'm so sorry.

JIM: You look like Harry, a boy I went to school with.

DELLA: Oh, I wished I'd never done it!

JIM: *(Intrigued)* No, no, it's all right.

DELLA: No, it ain't! You're just saying that!

JIM: No, I'm not. In fact, now that I get used to it a bit…I like it.

DELLA: *(Surprised)* You do?

JIM: *(Nods)* I do!

DELLA: *(Elated)* Oh, Jim!

(DELLA *hugs* JIM, *after a beat, still in the hug.*)

JIM: Della? I've got an idea.

DELLA: Yes?

JIM: Why don't you put on my clothes?

(DELLA *pulls out of the hug.*)

DELLA: *(Stunned)* What…?

JIM: Yes. Put on my suit and tie and everything.

DELLA: *(Confused)* Are you funning with me, Jim?

JIM: No. It's Christmas Eve. We can't use our gifts, so, why not? It'll be something different to do.

DELLA: *(Reluctantly)* Well. All right. If you want me to. *(She slowly stands and facing front, begins to unbutton her collar.)*

JIM: And I can put on your dress.

(DELLA *stops unbuttoning her collar.*)

DELLA: What?!

JIM: *(Excited)* And your stockings. And your underthings. And I'll even put on your makeup! And you can call me…"Mary Anne" and I'll call you… "Harry"!

DELLA: *(Utterly confused)* Wha…?

JIM: Oh, this is going to be a dandy Christmas, Della! Or should I say…Harry?

(Music: Same music as intro to scene and lights fade.)

Scene Nine

(Music fades as lights come up.)

(Another sidewalk)

(CHARMIAN and JOHN slowly walk on, from left, upstage, both holding paper cups.)

CHARMIAN: *(Sips drink)* Mmmmm… This is better than heroin.

JOHN: Told ya.

CHARMIAN: I bet you could O D on this. This could kill Keith Richards.

(CHARMIAN walks downstage towards "window" and JOHN follows.)

CHARMIAN: *(Sighs)* Oh, groan… The Greatest Generation's Christmas. Okay, I am so tired of them; "*We* survived the depression, *we* beat Hitler, *we* built the pyramids." When will they all just go away?

(Off JOHN's look)

CHARMIAN: Kidding. I love each and everyone of them. *(Looking at window)* And I love this living room. Reminds me of my Gramma's.

When is this supposed to be? During the war or after?

JOHN: I'd say it's…December twenty-fourth, nineteen forty-four, 11:35 P M.

CHARMIAN: *(Turns to him)* Go, Sherlock.

JOHN: *(Points at window)* There's a clock and a calendar on the wall.

CHARMIAN: Oh. *(She looks back at window)* Do you think Christmases were better back then?

JOHN: I don't know. It must've been scary, wondering who was going to win the war, if someone was coming home or not.

CHARMIAN: *(Low-key, real)* Yeah. I remember Christmas in Iraq.

JOHN: *(Playing along)* You were in Iraq?

CHARMIAN: I don't like to talk about it. Hey? Do you think they'll ever do a Christmas window about the war right now?

JOHN: Hard to believe that people will be nostalgic for "now".

CHARMIAN: *(Looks back at window, points)* Those two kids look exactly like my brother and me. We'd sneak downstairs to wait for Santa and we'd *always* fall asleep in front of the fireplace.

JOHN: One year my sister and I woke up really early, before my parents were awake and went down to the living room and we opened every single present. Finally they heard us and came down and we were sitting there and they'd missed the whole thing. My mother started crying. My dad yelled at us.

CHARMIAN: Y'know for the happiest day of the year, there's always a lot of yelling and crying.

(JOHN nods in agreement. They sip their hot chocolate.)

CHARMIAN: My parents made my brother and I wait at the top of the stairs, on Christmas morning, and there'd be a red ribbon strung up across so we couldn't go down until my mother cut it. Then we'd run down to the tree. And we *still* do it. My parents actually made us do it last year. Two adults waiting behind a stupid red ribbon. *(She turns back to window)* Can you read the names on their stockings? *(She leans forward, reading)* "Buddy" and...

(JOHN leans closer to look. Their shoulders touch. They don't move away from each other.)

JOHN: ..."Betty".

CHARMIAN: "Buddy and Betty". How cute is that? Why is there a blue star up in the window?

JOHN: That means they had somebody in the service, and if they got killed, they changed it to a gold star. They even had this song called "When A Blue Service Star Turns to Gold."

CHARMIAN: That is too sad. *(Then...)* Are you a World War II geek that watches the History Channel all the time? Cuz that would be even sadder.

(JOHN stands back up and so does CHARMIAN.)

JOHN: No. I was doing research for a novel about World War II, but I didn't know what the hell I was writing about. "Write what you know".

CHARMIAN: Well, why don't you write about a guy who gets fired on Christmas Eve and meets a beautiful, fascinating, talented, smart, funny girl and he tells her he's not an axe murderer, but, it turns out he really is. But then, we find out that she is too. And they live happily ever after killing people with their axes. The End. There. You got your best seller.

JOHN: I'll start on that tomorrow.

CHARMIAN: Well, you do have some "free time".

(Off JOHN*'s look)*

CHARMIAN: Too soon?

JOHN: I could do that. If I didn't eat or pay rent or pay student loans or my VISA bill or the money my parents lent me.

*(*CHARMIAN *sips the last of her hot chocolate. Leaning her head back, tipping the cup all the way back, tapping the bottom of it with her fingers to get every last drop.)*

CHARMIAN: Yum. That was the best hot chocolate I have ever had. Sorry, Gramma.

JOHN: I can't finish mine.

CHARMIAN: Um… Could I? It is so amazing.

JOHN: Sure.

*(*JOHN *holds out his cup.* CHARMIAN *starts to pour the rest of his into her cup. Hesitates)*

CHARMIAN: You don't have, like, leprosy do you?

JOHN: Just a little bit.

CHARMIAN: It's worth it. *(Pours it and sips)* I think I'm going to marry this hot chocolate.

JOHN: You better tell your boyfriend.

*(*JOHN *glances at his watch,* CHARMIAN *notices.)*

CHARMIAN: Do you have to get to your party?

JOHN: Eventually.

CHARMIAN: So, what kind of party is it? Wine, women, cock fights, jousting, human sacrifices?

JOHN: No, it'll be too many people in a tiny apartment getting drunk as fast as they can, desperately trying to have a good time with the *Charlie Brown Christmas* C D playing in the background—

CHARMIAN: Wait! Wait! I forgot! *A Charlie Brown Christmas!* How could I forget *A Charlie Brown Christmas*? That goes on my top five Christmas movie list. Number One.

JOHN: Uh, you can't put that on the list.

(CHARMIAN *looks at* JOHN *for second, surprised.*)

CHARMIAN: You don't like *A Charlie Brown Christmas*? *Everybody* likes *A Charlie Brown Christmas*. It's against the *law* not to like *A Charlie Brown Christmas*.

JOHN: No, I like it, but it's not a movie. It's a T V special. Wasn't it the Five Best Christmas *Movies* list?

CHARMIAN: *(Considers, a little miffed)* Yes, Mr. Rules & Regulations. It was. You are right. And I am wrong. I stand corrected. And I'm a big enough person to admit it. Are you?

JOHN: *(Laughs, slightly confused)* What?

CHARMIAN: *A Charlie Brown Christmas* shall be stricken from the list. *(Then)* Y'know, I can do the dances.

JOHN: What dances?

CHARMIAN: The Charlie Brown Christmas dances. You know, they're supposed to be rehearsing for the Christmas play and they just want to dance?

JOHN: I haven't seen it in—

(*Off* JOHN's *quizzical look,* CHARMIAN *puts down her cup and purse, looks around to make sure no one is watching.*)

(CHARMIAN *does the different dances that the Peanuts characters do—she does them expertly; a)* arms held out straight a la "Frankenstein" and walking in place; b) doing "The Pony" with her feet, with hands up, titling her head side to side; c) feet moving, not turning body, but turning head side to side, touching shoulder with chin.)

JOHN: Right. I remember—

CHARMIAN: I'm not done. *(She continues. She starts to look queasy. She stops.)* Okay. I'm done.

(JOHN claps.)

CHARMIAN: You're welcome.

JOHN: You're really good at that.

CHARMIAN: I know. *(Puts her hand on her stomach)* I...I think I drank too much Monsieur Hot Chocolate.

JOHN: You okay?

CHARMIAN: Do they have any stomach pump stores on this street?

JOHN: You want to get something? Like Pepto Bismal? There's a Duane Reed down this way.

CHARMIAN: Okay. Then can we go find Monsieur Chocolate and kill him?

JOHN: Sure.

CHARMIAN: *(As they walk off)* Bye, Buddy and Betty. Hitler loses.

(Lights fade.)

(Music: Perhaps White Christmas *or* Toyland *or a 40s-style version of* First Noel.*)*

Scene Ten

(Music fades out and lights come up.)

(BUDDY, 6 years old, BETTY, 4 years old, Both are asleep on the floor, lying against each other. Both are in 1940s style pajamas, robe, and slippers. She is holding a beat up Raggedy Ann doll. He wears a leather World War II Aviator cap.)

(BETTY wakes up.)

BETTY: Buddy? *(Louder, shakes him)* Buddy!

(Startled awake, BUDDY *pretends he was not asleep.)*

BUDDY: What? What do you want?

BETTY: You fell asleep.

BUDDY: No, I didn't.

BETTY: Yes, you did!

BUDDY: Shh! You're gonna wake up Mom.

BETTY: I heard a reindeer.

BUDDY: Aw, Betty, you're crazy. You don't even know what reindeer sound like.

BETTY: *(Worried)* Maybe it was Mommy. If she finds us down here she's gonna be mad. She said if we snuck down to wait for Santa she'd spank us.

BUDDY: No, she won't. Dad's the only one that spanks us. And he's thousands of miles away. *(He looks up chimney.)*

BETTY: What do you want him to bring you?

BUDDY: I haven't exactly decided, yet. Either a Kraut's head or a Jap's ear.

BETTY: Ew! You want Santa to bring you an ear?

BUDDY: Shhh! No, stupid! Not, Santa. I was talking about Dad.

BETTY: Oh… Do you think Daddy'll be here next Christmas?

BUDDY: Sure he will.

BETTY: What do you want Santa to bring you?

BUDDY: I told you a million times. A Gene Autry repeating cap pistol and the holster, too. *(Looks up chimney)* And I better get it this time.

BETTY: Y'know what I want Santa to bring me?

BUDDY: I hope he brings you a new doll. *(He grabs doll.)* This one stinks.

(BUDDY tosses doll aside. BETTY howls. He quickly grabs doll and gives it back to stop her crying.)

BETTY: She does not stink!

BUDDY: Shh! She does, too. Tell Mom to put her in the washing machine.

BETTY: No! Then she'll drown and die.

BUDDY: No, she won't, stupid. She's a doll. Dolls can't die.

(BETTY thinks about this.)

(BUDDY looks up chimney.)

BETTY: Buddy?

BUDDY: What?

BETTY: What if he doesn't come?

BUDDY: Santa always comes.

BETTY: I mean Daddy. What if he doesn't come back? What if Hitler shoots him?

BUDDY: Hitler ain't gonna shoot him. And even if he tried to, Dad'd shoot him first.

BETTY: Really?

BUDDY: Yeah. And then Dad'd come back home and I bet they'd give him a big parade and he'd get a medal and he'd even get to meet the president.

BETTY: Would he get to meet the president's dog?

BUDDY: Prob'ly.

Buddy looks up chimney.

BETTY: I wish we had a dog. *(Excited)* Maybe Santa'll bring us a dog!

BUDDY: Shhh! Mom says we can't get a dog until Dad comes home.

BETTY: She better tell Santa that.

Buddy yawns, then looks up the chimney, listening.

BETTY: Buddy?

BUDDY: *Now* what?

BETTY: Sarah Feldman…a girl…at my school…in my class, said Santa wasn't real.

BUDDY: Aw, she has to say that.

BETTY: Why?

BUDDY: She's Jewish.

BETTY: What's Jewish?

BUDDY: They don't believe in Santa Claus.

BETTY: Oh…Sarah Feldman said Hitler doesn't like her… Is that because she doesn't believe in Santa Claus? …Do you think Santa will bring anything to Hitler for Christmas? …What if Hitler asks Santa for a special gun to shoot Daddy?

BUDDY: Will you stop asking dumb questions and be quiet—! *(Suddenly holds still)* Did you hear that?

BETTY: What?

BUDDY: I heard something.

BETTY: What?

BUDDY: It sounded like…reindeer.

(BETTY *and* BUDDY *both listen intently.*)

(*Music: Same as intro to scene.*)

(*Lights fade.*)

Scene Eleven

(Music fades as lights come up.)

(Another sidewalk)

(CHARMIAN, looking queasy, and JOHN enter, she carries a bag from Duane Reade and a small Pepto Bismal bottle.)

JOHN: How do you feel?

CHARMIAN: The opposite of fantastic.

JOHN: Do you want to go home?

CHARMIAN: I don't know. Maybe I should.

JOHN: *(Disappointed)* Okay. *(Starts to walk off)* I'll get a taxi.

(CHARMIAN reaches out to stop JOHN.)

CHARMIAN: Wait. I…I'm not sure about being in a moving vehicle right now. Let's see if Pepto Bismal can work it's magic.

JOHN: Okay.

CHARMIAN: Sorry I had to run out of the store. The smell was making me feel worse than the hot chocolate.

JOHN: Yeah. What was that? It smelled like sour milk and rotten eggs—

CHARMIAN: *(Making her feel worse)* Uh, we really don't need to describe it—

JOHN: Sorry.

(CHARMIAN puts Pepto Bismal bottle and bag in her purse.)

CHARMIAN: This stuff used to always make me throw up.

(JOHN subtly backs away from CHARMIAN.)

CHARMIAN: When I was a kid. Don't worry. I'm not gonna throw up on Fifth Avenue.

JOHN: You'd be in good company, F Scott Fitzgerald did it a lot.

CHARMIAN: Yeah? And where is he today?

JOHN: Saint Mary's Cemetery. Rockville, Maryland. Section One. Aisle three, plot forty-seven.

CHARMIAN: Do I want to know why you know that?

JOHN: Well, I used to—now, this is extremely lame, but, keep in mind I was like thirteen or fourteen…or seventeen; I lived near Rockville and I used to go to his grave on weekends and read my short stories out loud.

CHARMIAN: I could see doing that. If I wanted to be a writer and liked Fitzgerald and was mentally unbalanced.

(CHARMIAN *and* JOHN *walk downstage. She looks up, as if reading a sign above the store window.*)

CHARMIAN: *(With slight dread)* "Christmas Around the World". Oh no, I think we're going to learn something. I don't want to learn anything. I just want to look at pretty windows. *(Reads plaque)* "In Ireland, on Christmas Eve, candles are placed on the windowsills so that Mary and Joseph, looking for shelter, may find the way to their homes and the front door is left open to welcome them."

JOHN: Well, this couple is following tradition. Door's wide open even though it's snowing.

CHARMIAN: I love when it snows on Christmas. I also love Mister Irish Man's sweater, which I bet is amazingly expensive.

JOHN: Yeah. I bought a jacket here once. I'm still paying for it.

CHARMIAN: Do you think this couple, living in their little one-room stone cottage in Ireland, could afford that sweater?

JOHN: I don't think they could afford anything in this store. But, c'mon, the ultimate goal of all these windows is to get people in the stores spending money.

CHARMIAN: Yeah, I know, but that doesn't bother me. For me, the best thing about Christmas is, you get to sit in a room with the people you love and you all give neat stuff to each other, 'cause you love 'em. I mean, how great is that? *(Beat…in a child's, crackly, Linus-Peanuts voice)* And that's why I love Christmas, Charlie Brown. *(Then mutters to herself, snarly)* Unless you don't get a god damned Barbie.

(JOHN smiles.)

JOHN: Feeling better?

CHARMIAN: Fifty-six percent better?

JOHN: You want to go on?

CHARMIAN: Neither rain, sleet, nor toxic hot chocolate will keep me from seeing these windows.

JOHN: *(Pleased)* Good.

CHARMIAN: *(As they walk off, over her shoulder to window)* Merry Christmas, Irish people. Erin go bragh.

(Lights fade and music up: Irish version of Wexford Carol *or* A Breton Carol *or* I Saw Three Ships.*)*

Scene Twelve

(Music fades out as lights come up.)

(Sitting in two plain, wooden chairs are CATHLEEN, *plain blouse, long skirt, shawl around her shoulders, knitting a scarf and* JOHNNY PAT, *in a sweater, cap, trousers, boots, arms crossed, staring off. She rarely looks at him, concentrating on her knitting.)*

CATHLEEN: Did you notice that sweet couple, Johnny Pat?

JOHNNY PAT: I suppose I did, Cathleen. Did you notice the weather we're havin'?

CATHLEEN: Aye. Cold. Remember when we used to go walking like that?

JOHNNY PAT: No. I can't say I do. Did you notice the wind blowing?

CATHLEEN: Aye. Blowing hard. You don't remember how we used to go walking together, now?

JOHNNY PAT: No. I don't remember. Do you see the snow coming down?

CATHLEEN: Aye. Christmas means snow. Yes, you do remember walking. We use to go walking all the time.

JOHNNY PAT: We never went walking, Cathleen.

CATHLEEN: Never went walking, you say? So tell me this, then, who was that fella I was walking with all that time?

JOHNNY PAT: I couldn't tell you. I wasn't there.

CATHLEEN: You were there, Johnny Pat. It was you walking with me.

JOHNNY PAT: But, Cathleen, I don't like to walk.

CATHLEEN: Not *now* you don't like to walk. But, you use to like to walk.

JOHNNY PAT: I never liked to walk.

(CATHLEEN *shakes her head and knits.*)

JOHNNY PAT: Returning now to me first inquiry regarding the weather; tell me this, then, if it's freezin' cold and the snow is falling and the wind is blowin', why do we have the front door wide open?

CATHLEEN: You know as well as I, Johnny Pat. We have to leave the door open for Mary and Joseph.

JOHNNY PAT: Do you mean crazy Mary McLoughlin who talks to dogs? And Old Jo Kelly who wets himself in church and calls it holy water?

CATHLEEN: No. I do not. That would be Bible Mary and Joseph that I am speaking of.

JOHNNY PAT: But, what if somebody else comes in? What if their names aren't Mary and Joseph? What if their names are Jack and Smacker and they rob us blind?

CATHLEEN: No one's robbin' us blind on Christmas Eve, now.

JOHNNY PAT: I would. It would be a grand time to do it. The front door is wide open. (*He mimes being stiff.*) People inside are frozen stiff so they couldn't do anything. Walk right in and steal whatever you wanted.

CATHLEEN: And what is it they would be stealing now, in this house?

(JOHNNY PAT *comes out of his "stiff" position and looks around, then looks down at his sweater.*)

JOHNNY PAT: Me sweater for one thing. A thief would be pleased to get his hands on such a sweater as this one. That girl, with the funny hat, she knew it was a grand sweater.

CATHLEEN: Aye. It is. I wish I had a sweater half as grand.

JOHNNY PAT: Do you, now? Do you know what I wish? I wish I had ten sweaters like this one.

CATHLEEN: And what would you be doing with ten sweaters, now?

JOHNNY PAT: Well, I'll tell ya, Cathleen. I'd be wearing 'em. All ten of 'em... *(He turns towards her in his chair and leans forward.)* ...because some feckin' loon has the feckin' front door open and I'm feckin' freezin' me arse off!

CATHLEEN: *(Calmly)* Johnny Pat, don't be swearing now. I won't be having you swearing on Christmas Eve.

JOHNNY PAT: I'll be feckin' swearing if I want to be feckin' swearing. You're not me feckin' mother!

CATHLEEN: I know I'm not your mother, God rest her soul.

JOHNNY PAT: Well, you're acting like me mother, and you're sounding like me mother, and if the truth be told, you're even starting to look like me mother!

(CATHLEEN stops knitting and looks at JOHNNY PAT.)

CATHLEEN: Johnny Pat, your mother was an angel on earth. A kinder soul never lived. A saint for sure. But, truth be told, she had a face like a bulldog chewing a wasp. She was the ugliest thing I ever saw in all me days.

(JOHNNY PAT stands and stomps his foot.)

CATHLEEN: She was, Johnny Pat, and you know it, and she knew it, and Jesus knows it and God knows it. So, I won't be having you saying I look like her. No one's going to be mistakin' me for Miss Marilyn Monroe, but that dog over there looks more like your mother than I do. And if your mother was here, she would say we need to keep the door open for Mary and Joseph.

JOHNNY PAT: Cathleen...I've got some interesting news for you. Mary and Joseph ain't coming here. And you want to be knowing why they won't be coming? *(Beat)* BECAUSE THEY BEEN DEAD FOR TWO THOUSAND FECKIN' YEARS!

CATHLEEN: I'm not an eejit, Johnny Pat. I know they're not really coming here. But, symbolically they are, so that's why we leave the door open.

(JOHNNY PAT *stares at* CATHLEEN *for a moment, shakes his head.*)

JOHNNY PAT: *(Looks off, sighs)* I use to like Christmas. When I was a wee one. Christmas is better when you're a wee one. Putting out your little sack by the fireplace so Santa would fill it up with toys and candy. That was nice.

CATHLEEN: Ay. It was nice.

(JOHNNY PAT *motions for her to lean over closer to him. She does.*)

JOHNNY PAT: Now, don't be telling this to anyone.

CATHLEEN: Don't be telling what?

JOHNNY PAT: Don't be telling nobody what I'm about to tell you.

CATHLEEN: If you're asking me not to tell, I won't tell, Johnny Pat.

JOHNNY PAT: You swear to Jesus?

CATHLEEN: I swear to Jesus.

JOHNNY PAT: And to your good pals, we're freezin' our arses off for, Mary and Joseph?

CATHLEEN: Ay!

JOHNNY PAT: Say it!

CATHLEEN: *(Sighs)* I swear to Jesus, Mary and Joseph, I won't be telling.

(JOHNNY PAT *leans over and whispers.*)

JOHNNY PAT: *(Quietly)* I wish...I wish I could put out a sack tonight for Santa and get some toys and candy in the morning.

(CATHLEEN *stares at* JOHNNY PAT.)

CATHLEEN: Are you drunk Johnny Pat?

JOHNNY PAT: No! Feck it! Shouldn't have told you!

CATHLEEN: What're you wishing for Santa to bring you toys and candy? If you're wanting toys and candy you can go buy toys and candy yourself, now.

JOHNNY PAT: I know I can buy toys and candy meself!

CATHLEEN: So why don't you then?

JOHNNY PAT: It's not the same!

CATHLEEN: But how else are you going to get them? Santa's not going to be bringing you no candy and toys, I hope you know that. And why you would be wanting toys at your age, I don't know. If I told people that you wanted toys—

(JOHNNY PAT *stands and looms over* CATHLEEN, *menacingly, pointing his finger at her.*)

JOHNNY PAT: You forget what I said about toys and candy! And I swear to Jesus and Joseph and Mary and whoever the feck else may be symbolically coming in that door, if you ever say a word, or breathe a syllable to man or woman or animal or insect or a rock lying in the road, I'll make sure you're laying next to me mother in her coffin staring at her hideous, horrible face for all eternity!

(CATHLEEN *and* JOHNNY PAT *stare at each other for a moment.*)

CATHLEEN: *(Calmly)* I won't be telling, Johnny Pat.

(JOHNNY PAT *nods. He sits. He composes himself.* CATHLEEN *knits again.*)

CATHLEEN: If you wanted me to, I'd put out a sack of toys and candy for you.

JOHNNY PAT: *(Slowly turns to look at her, surprised)* You would?

CATHLEEN: I would.

JOHNNY PAT: And you wouldn't be telling no one you did?

CATHLEEN: No. I wouldn't be telling no one. *(Beat. She knits.)*

JOHNNY PAT: I think I remember walking with you.

(CATHLEEN smiles to herself as she knits.)

(Lights fade.)

(Music: Same as intro to Scene)

Scene Thirteen

(Music fades and lights up.)

(Another sidewalk)

(CHARMIAN and JOHN enter, he holds a bag of roasted chestnuts, which they are both eating.)

CHARMIAN: …and as soon as someone finished opening the last gift, my brother would stand up and say, "Christmas… *(Pause)* …is over." And I'd burst out crying. Then my father would yell at my brother for making me cry and my mother would yell at my father for yelling at my brother and then my brother and I would start laughing at our parents… It was great. *(Holds out a chestnut)* Who knew that roasted chestnuts could cure an upset tummy? It's a Christmas miracle.

JOHN: I think Pepto Bismal deserves some credit, too.

CHARMIAN: John, why do you have to ruin my Christmas miracle?

JOHN: Sorry, I just—

(CHARMIAN's *cell rings: "I Still Haven't Found What I'm Looking For".*)

CHARMIAN: God, I hate that song. *(To* JOHN, *re phone call)* Sorry.

(JOHN *moves away to give* CHARMIAN *privacy.)*

CHARMIAN: *(Into phone, distracted)* Hey, Michael...Still looking at windows... Well, there's a lot of windows... Oh, yeah? What kind of surprise? ...

I don't want to guess... No, just tell me... Okay, uh, Santa's giving me a lead role in a Broadway play... Better? What's better than that?... *(Gobsmacked)* What? Are you serious? ...How'd you... What time is my flight? ...In the morning? That's really early...Well, yeah, I'm excited, but— It's just, I didn't expect to be flying home tomorrow morning... No, no. I can do it. Thank you, that's really sweet... Yeah...I gotta get back to my apartment, I gotta pack and do a million things... Thanks... Bye. *(Hangs up, to* JOHN*)* I don't believe it. Michael just bought me a plane ticket home tomorrow morning for Christmas.

JOHN: *(He so doesn't mean it)* Oh. That's great.

CHARMIAN: He said they had some crazy sale online because oddly enough no one likes to fly at 6:15 AM on Christmas Day... Oh my god, I'll have to get up in, like— *(Looks at her watch)* —four hours to go to the airport. I should probably get back and start packing.

JOHN: Yeah, I should probably get to my party before it ends.

CHARMIAN: Yeah.

JOHN: *(Points downstage)* Should we see the last window? Since we're here.

CHARMIAN: Um... Yeah. We kinda have to. It is Macy's. The King God of All Christmas Windows.

(CHARMIAN *and* JOHN *approach window and look at it for a beat.*)

CHARMIAN: Oh...I hate this story. This is the saddest story in the world. Why would they do a window of this?

JOHN: Well, it is a classic Christmas story.

CHARMIAN: It's a classic Christmas downer. Little girl standing in the snow, barefoot, trying to sell matches. She can't. She lights all her matches. She hallucinates. She dies. Merry Christmas! ...Who wrote it?

JOHN: Hans Christian Anderson.

CHARMIAN: Well, Mister Hans Christian Anderson should have been shot for writing that story.

JOHN: Shot?

CHARMIAN: *(Reconsiders)* Well, in the foot.

JOHN: Well, in Hans's defense, I think he was trying to make a point.

CHARMIAN: Don't stand barefoot in the snow and sell matches?

JOHN: No. He was reminding people that during the holidays there are people suffering, there's poverty and you should be charitable and help the poor. *(Looks at window)* She reminds people that everyone doesn't live happily ever after. Everybody's dreams don't come true. With a happy ending, you feel good; whereas if it's a sad ending hopefully you're inspired to do something about the problem. Or at least think about it. Or talk about it. Like we're doing a hundred and fifty years later.

CHARMIAN: *(To window, reluctantly)* Okay, you are absolved Little Match Girl. You have a higher purpose.

JOHN: I mean, that's great writing.

CHARMIAN: Maybe you'll write something like that.

JOHN: No. That's not going to happen.

CHARMIAN: C'mon, maybe the new book you're working on will be the one? Fourth times the charm.

JOHN: No. I read it today, after I left the office, sitting in a Starbucks, and it was really, really bad.

CHARMIAN: I bet it wasn't "really, really bad".

JOHN: Trust me. It was really, really bad. It was so really, really bad I threw it away.

CHARMIAN: You did not.

JOHN: I did. And you know what? It felt great.

CHARMIAN: Wait, but, you have it on your computer, right?

JOHN: No. I write my first drafts in pencil. (*Mocking himself*) Because Fitzgerald did.

(CHARMIAN *grabs his arm.*)

CHARMIAN: Where'd you throw it away?

JOHN: At the Starbucks.

CHARMIAN: We gotta go get it!

JOHN: Why?

CHARMIAN: Stephen King!

JOHN: Stephen King?

CHARMIAN: Stephen King thought his first novel was a piece of shit and threw it away. His wife, Tabitha, pulled it out of the trash, told him to finish it and it got published. True story.

(JOHN *looks at* CHARMIAN *for a moment.*)

JOHN: I don't like Stephen King.

CHARMIAN: That's not the point! (*Starts to drag him off*) C'mon, we gotta go get it.

JOHN: We're never going to find it.

CHARMIAN: Not if we don't look!

JOHN: It could take forever.

CHARMIAN: If we look badly. I plan to look with skill and precision.

JOHN: We can't look through the trash, we'll catch some disease.

CHARMIAN: Sometimes you have to suffer for art.

JOHN: Trust me we're not looking for art. Look, I appreciate it, Charmian, but it's not worth it.

CHARMIAN: You don't know that!

JOHN: You don't either! Don't you have to go home and pack?

CHARMIAN: Eventually. But we can still do this.

JOHN: You said you had to go the airport in like four hours—

CHARMIAN: I'll just stay up—

JOHN: Charmian, this is stupid. It's a dumb idea.

(CHARMIAN *turns away from* JOHN.)

CHARMIAN: Fine. Never mind. Forget it.

JOHN: Charmian—

CHARMIAN: I have to go home and pack. I'm going to get a cab.

JOHN: Charmian, wait, look, I really appreciate it, I mean, that you'd want to do that, but, why would you want to go through the trash for some half-finished thing that could be worthless.

(CHARMIAN *turns to* JOHN. *As serious as she's been all night.*)

CHARMIAN: *(Quietly)* Because I don't think people should quit doing what they really want to do and give up.

JOHN: You've never read anything I've written. I could suck. I could be a horrible writer. They could all be right; all the publishers, my old girlfriends—

CHARMIAN: And they could be wrong, too. Maybe you wrote something amazing that's going to last as long as… *(Nods to window)* …Little Miss Matchy and her terribly depressing story of death and tragedy, that nonetheless relays an important message.

JOHN: I don't think so.

CHARMIAN: Let's find out.

(CHARMIAN grabs JOHN's arm and pulls him off.)

(Lights fade out.)

(Music: Sad, melancholy version on piano or violin of What Child Is This?*)*

Scene Fourteen

(Music fades as lights come up.)

(LITTLE MARCH GIRL facing audience. Barefoot, tattered dress, long hair, holding out a box of matches.)

LITTLE MATCH GIRL: *(Tough, street-wise, a stuffed up nose)* That lady is right. Why do I have to be the one to remind people that everybody doesn't live happily ever after? I don't want to die. *(Sniffles. Wipes her nose with hand. She spots a cigarette on the ground. Picks it up.)* I know I shouldn't. I'm too young. I'm eight. I think. *(Lights cigarette and smokes.)* But, I'll be dead soon. I'm never going to be old enough to smoke. Might as well have a little experience in my short pathetic life. *(Puffs)* I bet that man wouldn't want to die a horrible death just to remind somebody that people get run over by carriages or drown or get some disease…I'd like to see him stand in the snow, barefoot, and try and sell matches. *(Puffs)* I wish I could beg. They arrest you for that. It's illegal. You can't beg. The coppers get you. So I have to sell matches… My sister sells her lady parts. She makes a lot of money. And she doesn't have to stand outside in the snow. She gets to be inside in a nice, warm, soft bed. *(Puff)* Nobody asked me if I wanted to serve a greater purpose. It's not fair. I want a happy ending. I want a rich man to pull up in a carriage and say, "Come with me to my home and you shall be warm and dry and eat roast goose with apple and plum stuffing and all the presents under the Christmas tree are yours and you shall wear beautiful clothes and you shall never have to stand in the snow and sell matches ever again." *(She takes a puff. Coughs. Puts out cigarette)*

(Her tough persona begins to soften. She sits down on the ground. She lights a match, puts her hand over it to warm herself.)

LITTLE MATCH GIRL: I don't want to be The Little Match Girl. *(She lies down on the ground, still holding the match, looking at the flame as it illuminates her face.)* I want to be Cinderella…or Snow White…or Sleeping Beauty…I want to live happily ever after.

*(*LITTLE MARCH GIRL *stares at the match flame. It goes out. Darkness)*

(Music: Same as intro to Scene.)

Scene Fifteen

(Lights up. Music fades.)

(Another sidewalk, near a Starbucks)

(JOHN stands. CHARMIAN sits on the platform upstage. She is intently reading from a wet, coffee stained spiral notebook.)

(She reads for a bit, then looks up at him.)

CHARMIAN: *(Serious)* John, this is really good.

JOHN: You don't have to say that.

CHARMIAN: *(Slightly offended)* I'm not. I read a lot. I know what's good. This is really good.

JOHN: Thanks.

(CHARMIAN closes notebook.)

CHARMIAN: And I'm glad it's really good because if we'd spent all that time going through that trash and it sucked, I'd be really pissed. *(Holds notebook out to him)* You have to finish this. I probably got the plague finding this, so if I die tomorrow it better be for something.

JOHN: Okay. *(He reluctantly takes it.)*

CHARMIAN: And when it gets published you have to dedicate it to me. And make sure you spell my name right or I'll sue. *(Serious)* You are going to finish it, right?

JOHN: *(Sighs)* I'll try.

CHARMIAN: No! *(As Yoda)* "Do. Or do not. There is no try." Seriously, promise me you're going to finish it. Say it. Raise your right hand.

(JOHN halfheartedly raises his hand.)

JOHN: I promise.

CHARMIAN: Okay. And that's a Christmas Eve Promise. You *cannot* break it or Santa comes and kills you.

JOHN: Santa…kills you?

CHARMIAN: *(Matter-of-factly)* Yes. Little know Christmas tradition. They don't publicize it much.

JOHN: I can see why.

CHARMIAN: So you wanna split a cab?

JOHN: I'm in Brooklyn, so I'm subway.

CHARMIAN: Okay.

(JOHN puts notebook in bag. Sees something in there.)

JOHN: Oh. Hey. I know you're violently opposed to opening gifts on Christmas Eve, but, I got you something. Didn't have time to wrap it. *(He pulls out a Barbie doll in a box.)*

(CHARMIAN, for once, is almost speechless.)

CHARMIAN: Oh my god…I don't believe it. This is… Where'd you get this?

JOHN: At the Duane Reed after you ran out.

CHARMIAN: *(Looks at doll, genuinely touched)* I finally got a Barbie… *This* is the *greatest* Christmas gift ever. This is… It's amazingly amazing… Thank you.

JOHN: You're welcome.

(CHARMIAN puts it in her purse.)

CHARMIAN: I'll have to sneak her in tomorrow when I go to my parent's house, so my mom doesn't see her— Oh, I gotta tell them I'm coming.

JOHN: So, how long are you going for?

CHARMIAN: *(Realizing)* Shit. Michael didn't tell me. Typical. Just a sec— *(Takes out cell and dials)* Hey… Michael, wait, you didn't tell me, when do I fly back to New York? …What? That's like two weeks…I can't

be away two weeks... Why not? I have to work, I
have auditions...I can't miss any auditions... No, I
can't... *(Coldly)* What's that suppose to mean? ...No. I
don't know. Tell me. *(She listens for a bit.)* Hey, I know
I haven't gotten any parts and I know how long I've
been here... Well, I think maybe it could happen...I
appreciate your rousing vote of confidence. I gotta go.
(She hangs up.)

*(CHARMIAN and JOHN both stand there for a moment.
Uncomfortable. Awkward moment. She knows he's heard
some of the conversation.)*

(She looks downstage.)

CHARMIAN: Hey... Bonus window. Not on the tour.

JOHN: *(Looks downstage)* Where?

CHARMIAN: *(Points left)* There. That little one.

*(CHARMIAN and JOHN walk downstage, standing close and
look at window.)*

CHARMIAN: I didn't know anybody did ones like this
anymore.

JOHN: Yeah. It is kind of surprising.

CHARMIAN: I wonder if they got any complaints?

JOHN: Probably.

CHARMIAN: Well, it is Christmas. I mean, why not? Can
I just say that Mary looks fabulous for someone who
just gave birth, in a stable, with no doctor, or drugs, or
Lamaze classes. *(Looks closer)* What's that stuff in the
box behind the donkey?

JOHN: I think that's the gold, frankincense and myrrh,
from the Wise Men.

CHARMIAN: What exactly is "myrrh"?

JOHN: I think it's dried tree sap.

CHARMIAN: Well, they totally re-gifted that.

JOHN: Hey, we should tell Mary and Joseph that there's a little Irish couple that's waiting to have a party for them.

CHARMIAN: Yeah. *(Looks at her watch)* Speaking of parties, you're going to be extremely fashionably late for yours.

JOHN: Yeah. You're going to miss yours. You have to pack.

CHARMIAN: Yeah. Well. Actually, I didn't have a party. When I meet somebody I always say I'm going to a party later, for a good escape plan, in case the person's a weirdo. But, you aren't a weirdo. You're a really nice person— Am I a weirdo?

(JOHN smiles.)

CHARMIAN: Yeah. I know. Too bad I can't get paid for it. *(She turns back to window.)* Well, Christmas Window Looking…is over.

JOHN: Hey. I had a great time. This was fun.

CHARMIAN: *And* educational, too; now I know all about blue stars and gold stars and where F Scott Fitzgerald's buried and why they write horribly depressing Christmas stories and where to get hot chocolate that makes you wanna throw up… Thanks for going with me.

JOHN: Thanks for inviting me.

CHARMIAN: I'll look for your name on the best seller list.

JOHN: Thanks. I'll look for your name up on a marquee.

CHARMIAN: Yeah. They won't spell it right.

(JOHN extends his hand and they awkwardly shake hands. Their hands remain together. John moves slightly closer as if to kiss her, then changes his mind and moves back.)

JOHN: Merry Christmas.

CHARMIAN: Yeah. Merry Christmas.

(Lights fade out on them, downstage left.)

(Music: Soft, solemn version of Silent Night. *Solo guitar or piano or voices.)*

Scene Sixteen

(Music fades out as lights fade up.)

*(*JOSEPH *and* MARY, *20s, in traditional, biblical garb. She is sitting, on a low stool, holding a baby in swaddling clothes. He stands behind her, a hand on her shoulder.)*

(Possible staging: JOSEPH *and* MARY *may be positioned upstage on a small platform.* CHARMIAN *and* JOHN *remain, in tableau, in the dark, downstage left.)*

MARY: Why didst the man not kiss the woman?

JOSEPH: Did thou thinketh he should have?

MARY: Ye, I say unto thee; she desireth it with all her heart.

JOSEPH: No, wife, thou art wrong.

MARY: Joseph, that was a "I desireth to be kissed" face. The man hath been foolish.

JOSEPH: No. The man hath been wise. Trusteth me. Thou must be wary of a woman's face. They may looketh as if they desireth to be kissed— *(Reliving the experience)* —but, lo, when thou does, they may striketh ones face and cry, "Joseph! Taketh thy wretched lips from mine! Thou makest me wish to vomit in the marketplace!" *(Slightly embarrassed at his outburst, composes himself)*

MARY: My husband, thou art wrong. Thou must *not* be wary; thou must taketh the chance or thou may miss the love of thy life. It is better to be struck and suffer curses than never knowest the truth. If I were not married to thee, I wouldst have kissed the man gladly.

JOSEPH: *(Surprised)* Thou wouldst?

MARY: *(Nods, then wistfully)* He remindeth me of the glorious angel that came unto me—

(JOSEPH rolls his eyes and shakes his head. He's heard this a million times.)

JOSEPH: *(Softly)* Oy.

MARY: —who shineth like a star, with hair of gold and eyes of fire—

JOSEPH: Yea. Thou hath told that tale. A multitude of times… Uh, Mary?

MARY: Yes, husband?

JOSEPH: That angel, thou said his name was "Gabriel"?

MARY: Yes.

JOSEPH: Art thou…*certain* he was an angel?

MARY: Yes, husband.

JOSEPH: But, verily I say unto you, could thou hath been visited, in truth, not by an angel, but by a man who *pretended* to be an angel?

(MARY turns to look up at JOSEPH, then outwards, blissfully.)

MARY: He was… *(Bites her lip)* …an *angel*.

(JOSEPH sighs. Reluctantly nods, she turns to look back to the babe in arms.)

JOSEPH: Wife, what does thou wish to do with thy gifts that have been bestowed upon us?

MARY: We shalt keep the frankincense and gold and giveth the myrrh to thy mother.

JOSEPH: *(Looks out window)* Hark! The man and woman speaketh.

(JOSEPH and MARY freeze as lights come up on CHARMIAN and JOHN downstage.)

(Music: Silent Night*)*

Scene Seventeen

(Music fades and lights up.)

(Same sidewalk as before)

(CHARMIAN and JOHN standing as before.)

CHARMIAN: I'm really glad you weren't an axe murderer, this wouldn't have been as much fun. At least for me. *Unless* you are an axe murderer and it's a big surprise ending?

JOHN: If I was an axe murderer, wouldn't I have an axe?

CHARMIAN: Could be in your bag.

(JOHN opens his bag up.)

JOHN: Only dangerous thing I have in here is… *(Pulls out a stapler)* …a stapler.

CHARMIAN: *(Serious, as if it was real)* Wait— Are you the famous Christmas Eve Staple Murderer, that goes around and staples people to death?

JOHN: *(Serious)* Yes. *(He raises stapler up like a knife)* "Just kidding". *(Smiles)* No. It was a souvenir from my old job. I don't know why I took it. I've got a stapler. You want it? *(Starts to hand it to her, then pulls his hand back)* You're not going to throw it at me?

CHARMIAN: No. *(She takes it from JOHN)* Wow. A Barbie *and* a stapler. This is one awesome Christmas.

This is like the one my mom uses to staple up the red ribbon. My dad gets so mad. There're all these little staple marks on the wall and every year he has to pull them out and spackle and paint. He always says, "Jenny! No staples! Use tape!" *(Beat, she takes a breath)* My mother actually sent me a red ribbon two days ago to put up in my apartment. She said, "I know you're going to be big and famous and make us all so proud, but you have to... remember to— *(She turns away from him.)*

JOHN: What?

(CHARMIAN begins to cry.)

JOHN: Charmian...? What's the matter?

CHARMIAN: *(Breaks down, crying)* I'm not gonna be a big, famous actor...I'm not even going to be a little, sort-of-famous actor. I've had twenty-three auditions since I got here and haven't got a single job. Not even a call-back... And yesterday, at an audition, when I finished, the casting person looked at me said, "Where're you from?" And I told them and they said, 'Honey, you're not ready for New York. Go back to Kokomo"...And he's right. And Michael's right. They're all right. I should go home. *(Takes a breath)* I'm just not that good.

JOHN: Charmian, you're a good actress.

CHARMIAN: No, I'm not.

JOHN: You are.

(CHARMIAN turns to look at JOHN.)

CHARMIAN: What...? You've never seen me act.

JOHN: I saw you do *Romeo & Juliet*.

(CHARMIAN shakes her head dismissively.)

JOHN: I know good acting. I see plays. You're good.

CHARMIAN: I wish you were a casting director.

JOHN: I need a job. Maybe that's what I'll do.

CHARMIAN: John, I've been here six months and nothing's happened.

JOHN: Yeah, but something could happen next week or next month.
You'll never know what could've happened if you leave.

CHARMIAN: I can't... Why are you doing this?

JOHN: Because somebody once said people shouldn't quit doing what they really want to do and give up.

CHARMIAN: Well, whoever told you that was full of shit.

(Beat)

JOHN: And I don't want you to go.

(CHARMIAN *tries to take this all in.*)

CHARMIAN: John, I just don't have what it takes.

JOHN: I know. You don't.

CHARMIAN: *(A bit offended, surprised)* What...?

JOHN: Give me the stapler.

CHARMIAN: *(Confused)* What...?

JOHN: Just give it to me.

(CHARMIAN *hands* JOHN *the stapler.*)

(*He takes it, puts under his arm, reaches into his bag, tears off two legal sized pages from a pad, staples the ends of paper together. He puts down his bag.*)

CHARMIAN: What are you— ?

(JOHN *then tears three small diagonal tears, about two inches, at a angle.*)

(*He has made a paper crown.*)

(As he places it on her head…)

JOHN: You are hereby crowned the new Queen of Actors.

(CHARMIAN is overwhelmed. Then…)

CHARMIAN: *(Softly, touched)* This is…a *really* shitty crown.

JOHN: You're welcome.

(CHARMIAN thinks for a moment. Takes a breath. Exhales)

CHARMIAN: Okay. I'll stay and become a big famous actor.

JOHN: It may take awhile… You better tell Mister Indiana.

CHARMIAN: Yeah…I better tell him some other things, too.

JOHN: *(Smiles)* Good.

CHARMIAN: But, you're staying, too, and becoming a big famous writer. You made a Christmas Promise. You don't want Santa coming and killing you.

JOHN: No. I don't.

(CHARMIAN and JOHN look at each other.)

CHARMIAN: I wish there were more windows.

JOHN: Me, too.

JOHN: You want to see if we can find some more?

CHARMIAN: Okay.

(JOHN picks up his bag. Faces CHARMIAN.)

JOHN: If I…kiss you right now are you going to punch me in the nose?

CHARMIAN: *(Shrugs)* I dunno. Let's find out.

(A sweet kiss. CHARMIAN and JOHN come out of it.)

(She suddenly makes a fist of her hand. Then…)

CHARMIAN: Just kidding.

(JOHN *does a "courtesy laugh", then offers his arm.*
CHARMIAN *takes it.*)

JOHN: Lead on MacDuff.

(*As* CHARMIAN *and* JOHN *walk off together.*)

CHARMIAN: "Lay on MacDuff". Didn't you learn
anything tonight?

(*Lights fade out.*)

Scene Eighteen

(*Lights up*)

(JOSEPH and MARY as before. She is looking off in the
direction CHARMIAN and JOHN exited.

(MARY *sighs, disappointed*)

JOSEPH: Why art thou sad, wife?

MARY: I shall not knoweth what happens to the man
and woman.

JOSEPH: What does thou wish to know?

MARY: Shall they join as one and have glad tidings and
joy? Or shall they suckle at the bitter vine of misery?

JOSEPH: One shalt never know what is to happen, as
the sun riseth from one day to the next. I wouldst think
that thou, of all women, knoweth that.

MARY: (*Nods*) I hope they shall dwell happily together
all their days.

JOSEPH: If that is thy hope, it shall be mine.

(JOSEPH *places his hand upon* MARY'*s shoulder.*)

(*She looks down at the babe in arms.*)

(*A pause...*)

(JOSEPH *thinks. He is still bothered by something. Finally he can longer contain himself.*)

JOSEPH: Art thou positive he was a—

MARY: YES!

(Black out!)

(Music: Joy To The World!*)*

END OF PLAY